READER'S PASSAGES
to accompany

ANALYTICAL READING INVENTORY

*Comprehensive Standards-Based Assessment
for All Students
Including Gifted and Remedial*

Eighth Edition

Mary Lynn Woods
University of Indianapolis

Alden J. Moe
Rollins College

PEARSON
Merrill
Prentice Hall

Upper Saddle River, New Jersey
Columbus, Ohio

Vice President and Executive Publisher: Jeffery W. Johnston
Senior Editor: Linda Ashe Bishop
Senior Production Editor: Mary M. Irvin
Design Coordinator: Diane C. Lorenzo
Project Coordination and Text Design: Lea Baranowski, Carlisle Editorial Services
Cover Design: Candace Rowley
Cover Image: SuperStock
Production Manager: Pamela D. Bennett
Director of Marketing: David Gesell
Marketing Manager: Darcy Betts Prybella
Marketing Coordinator: Brian Mounts

This book was set in Palatino by Carlisle Publishing Services. It was printed and bound by Banta. The cover was printed by Phoenix Color Corp.

Pearson Prentice Hall™ is a trademark of Pearson Education, Inc.
Pearson® is a registered trademark of Pearson plc
Prentice Hall® is a registered trademark of Pearson Education, Inc.
Merrill® is a registered trademark of Pearson Education, Inc.

Pearson Education Ltd.
Pearson Education Singapore Pte. Ltd.
Pearson Education Canada, Ltd.
Pearson Education—Japan

Pearson Education Australia Pty. Limited
Pearson Education North Asia Ltd.
Pearson Educación de Mexico, S.A. de C.V.
Pearson Education Malaysia Pte. Ltd.

10 9 8 7 6 5 4 3 2 1
ISBN 0-13-172347-2

Contents

Reader's Passages

◼ FORM A ◼

Word Lists and Narrative Passages, Preprimer—Nine

PRIMER	ONE	TWO
1. not	1. kind	1. mile
2. funny	2. rocket	2. fair
3. book	3. behind	3. ago
4. thank	4. our	4. need
5. good	5. men	5. fourth
6. into	6. met	6. lazy
7. know	7. wish	7. field
8. your	8. told	8. taken
9. come	9. after	9. everything
10. help	10. ready	10. part
11. man	11. barn	11. save
12. now	12. next	12. hide
13. show	13. cat	13. instead
14. want	14. hold	14. bad
15. did	15. story	15. love
16. have	16. turtle	16. breakfast
17. little	17. give	17. reach
18. cake	18. cry	18. song
19. home	19. fight	19. cupcake
20. soon	20. please	20. trunk

THREE	**FOUR**	**FIVE**	**SIX**
1. beginning	1. worm	1. abandon	1. seventeen
2. thankful	2. afford	2. zigzag	2. annoy
3. written	3. player	3. terrific	3. dwindle
4. reason	4. scientific	4. terrify	4. rival
5. bent	5. meek	5. plantation	5. hesitation
6. patient	6. rodeo	6. loaf	6. navigator
7. manage	7. festival	7. hike	7. gorge
8. arithmetic	8. hillside	8. relative	8. burglar
9. burst	9. coward	9. available	9. construction
10. bush	10. boom	10. grief	10. exploration
11. gingerbread	11. booth	11. physical	11. technical
12. tremble	12. freeze	12. commander	12. spice
13. planet	13. protest	13. error	13. spike
14. struggle	14. nervous	14. woodcutter	14. prevail
15. museum	15. sparrow	15. submarine	15. memorial
16. grin	16. level	16. ignore	16. initiation
17. ill	17. underground	17. disappointed	17. undergrowth
18. alarm	18. oxen	18. wrestle	18. ladle
19. cool	19. eighty	19. vehicle	19. walnut
20. engine	20. shouldn't	20. international	20. tributary

The Lost Candy

"I lost my candy," said the boy. "Help me find it."

"I see it," said Mom. "I see it in your hair! I will pull it out! Don't cry!"

Pat Hides Out

Pat sat by the tree. "Pat," his mom called. "I want you to help me," she said.

"I do not want to help her," Pat said to himself. "I do not want to work. I will hide from her. I will hide by this big tree! My mom will not find me."

The Crowded Car

Terry got into a little car. He had something for Show and Tell in a big paper bag. Next, Bill got into the car with his big paper bag.

Then Ann got into the car. She had something for Show and Tell in a big paper bag, too. Last, Sue got into the car with her big paper bag. Now, the little car was ready to go to school. "This little car is getting fat!" said Terry. The children laughed.

The Baseball Star

Whiz! The baseball went right by me, and I struck at the air! "Strike one," called the man. I could feel my legs begin to shake!

Whiz! The ball went by me again, and I began to feel bad. "Strike two," screamed the man.

I held the bat back because this time I would smack the ball! I would hit it right out of the park! I was so scared that I bit down on my lip. My knees shook and my hands grew wet. Swish! The ball came right over the plate. Crack! I hit it a good one! Then I ran like the wind. Everyone was yelling for me because I was now a baseball star.

Exploring a Cave

The sunlight shined into the mouth of the cave so Mark could see easily at first, but the farther he walked, the darker it grew. His dog, Boxer, ran off to explore on his own.

Soon it grew so dark that Mark could see nothing, but he could hear water dripping off the cave walls. He touched a wall with his hand to find it cold and damp. Mark began to grow fearful, so he lit his candle and held it high to look around.

Suddenly, the flame went out. He tried to relight the candle, but the first match went out! Finally, Mark's shaking hand held the lighted candle high. He heard a low growl near him and saw a pair of fierce, green eyes glowing in the dark! "Boxer!" he shouted. "Now I recognize those green eyes of yours! Let's get out of here!"

Crossing the River

The two dogs and the cat were growing tired from their long journey. Now they had to cross a river. It was wide and deep, so they would have to swim across.

The younger dog plunged into the icy water, barking for the others to follow him. The older dog jumped into the water. He was weak and suffering from pain, but somehow he managed to struggle to the opposite bank.

The poor cat was left alone. He was so afraid that he ran up and down the bank wailing with fear. The younger dog swam back and forth trying to help. Finally, the cat jumped in and began swimming near his friend.

At that moment something bad happened. A beaver dam from upstream broke. The water rushed downstream, hurling a large log toward the animals. It struck the cat and swept him helplessly away.

The Bicycle Race

"Look out," Sheila Young thought as she saw her challenger's bicycle come too close. "Watch out or you will foul me!"

At that moment a horrifying thing happened as she was bumped by another racer at forty miles an hour. Sheila's bicycle crashed, and she skidded on the surface of the track. From the wreck she received a nine-inch gash on her head.

The judges ruled that the race should be run again since a foul had been made. Sheila would not have enough time to get her wound stitched; still, she didn't want to quit the race because she could only think of winning. "Just staple the cut together and bandage it," she told the doctor. "I want to win this race!"

The doctor did as Sheila asked, and as she stood in silence while being treated, tears rolled down her face from the intense pain. Then, with a blood-stained bandage on her throbbing head, she pushed on to amaze the crowd with a sensational victory and a gold medal!

Remembering a Surgeon

It was a dreary April afternoon in 1950. Family, friends, and physicians from Freedmen's Hospital in Washington, D.C., gathered in the cemetery to attend the funeral of Dr. Charles Drew. After the burial two men stood off to the side talking in low, hushed voices.

"His research on blood transfusions saved the lives of thousands in war-torn Europe during World War II," one of the men remarked.

"He was an outstanding surgeon," the second man continued to add to the list of Drew's many accomplishments.

"Why did he attempt to drive the long distance from Washington to Alabama when he could have traveled by train?" the first man asked in a voice that revealed his deep sorrow.

"He had planned to take the train, but chose to drive because some fellow surgeons could not afford to take the train. He had been the honored speaker at a meeting the night before they left for the long car trip to Alabama. No one knew that he'd only had a few hours of sleep before starting out at two o'clock in the morning. No one realized that he was so tired."

Turning Himself In

While he had been hiding out for the past five days, Johnny had given serious thought to the whole mess. He had decided to return home, turn himself in to the police, and take the consequences of his crime. Being only sixteen, he was too young to run away for the rest of his life. He knew the fight had been in self-defense, but the fact still remained that he had killed another person, and the thought of that miserable night in the city park sent Johnny into a terrified panic.

He told Dally and Ponyboy of his decision, and now Dally reluctantly began the long drive home. Dally had gone to jail before, and this was one wretched experience he did not want his friend to have to endure.

As they reached the top of Jay Mountain, Dally slammed on the brakes! The old church where Johnny and Ponyboy had been hiding was in flames! Ponyboy and Johnny bolted from the car to question a bystander, who explained that they were having a school picnic when the church began to burn.

Suddenly, the crowd was shocked to hear desperate cries from inside! Ponyboy and Johnny ran into the burning church, and the boys lifted the children one by one through a window to safety. Chunks of the old roof were already beginning to fall as the last child was taken out. Ponyboy leaped through the window, vaguely hearing the sound of falling timber. Then, as he lay coughing and exhausted on the ground, he heard Johnny's terrifying scream!

Adjusting to a New School

Painfully shy, Jeffrey Vargus practically had to force himself off the school bus. "One step forward," he muttered in an attempt to convince himself to take on this awesome responsibility, "then eleven steps homeward where I can be stress-free working on my computer!" The problem of being a new student and having to make new acquaintances weighed heavily on his mind. Why did his parents have to move to a new town just as he was entering the eighth grade? Obviously reluctant, he trudged along at a less than enthusiastic pace toward the front door of Comstock Middle School.

Other students poured around him as if they were hurrying toward the building like a bunch of kids scampering toward ice cream and cake. "Every single student in the school knows everybody else, and nobody knows me, not a solitary soul!" Sweat began to drip from his forehead, causing his thick, dark-rimmed glasses to slide down his nose. "I'm returning home this instant," his head bellowed out the words, but not one came from his mouth. Suddenly, without warning, he spun around, thinking perhaps he'd escape into thin air. He dropped the book that had been tucked between his arm and chest like a security blanket. It smacked to the sidewalk, and he leaned forward to capture it from trampling feet.

"Hey, New Boy, you dropped your book!" a voice resounded so close to his ear that he stumbled backward. "*Computer Programming Tips for Whiz-Kid Teens!*" the voice read the title in a congenial manner. "Wow, are you interested in computer programming? Our school has the most elaborate computer lab in the entire county! Man, computer programming is my life's passion and challenge, so follow me. I'll show you the layout and introduce you to the other kids!"

The Crystal Clear Lake

"This magnificent lake contains treated sewer water!" the old gentleman murmured to himself as he sat on the park bench as close to the shore as possible. Leaning forward, his elbows resting on his knees, he looked out over the glistening water. The breeze across the lake caused the sailboats to glide about effortlessly, and in the distance he could see children entertaining themselves on the beach.

"We are making great environmental strides," he said quietly. He knew the history of this remarkable lake nestled in the foothills of southern California. He swelled with pride to recall the wise choice the Santee citizens had made when they voted not to support a disposal system that discharged waste directly into the Pacific Ocean. Rather, the citizens agreed to construct their own sewage facility, one that reclaimed the sewer water, spared the environment, and created community recreational opportunities.

"What an ingenious and environmentally conscious plan it was to build a city park just yards downstream from a sewer plant," the gentleman thought. He leaned forward and scooped up a handful of water. "This lake is more sanitary than many natural lakes! Inventive foresight and resourcefulness, that's what it took to make this unprecedented plan possible! Not only do the sewage waste solids furnish marketable soil conditioners and plant fertilizers, but the pure water provides lucrative recreational facilities!"

As the old gentleman got up, he saw dirty wrappers and other paper carelessly strewn over the walkways. "We demand it, use it, and thoughtlessly throw it away!" he muttered, and his contented expression changed to one of concern. His thoughts raced on as he bent forward to pick up the mess. "With such needless waste, how long can the world's resources continue to supply our reckless use? The United States comprises such a small percent of the world's population, yet we are the world's largest consumer of raw materials." He thought about this widespread behavior of consumption and waste, and as he discarded the paper into a nearby trash container, he wondered if things would ever change.

Reader's Passages

FORM B

Word Lists and Narrative Passages,
Preprimer—Nine

PRIMER	ONE	TWO
1. birthday	1. town	1. yet
2. went	2. bear	2. minute
3. fish	3. sound	3. act
4. like	4. party	4. bunny
5. something	5. there	5. empty
6. blue	6. these	6. inside
7. that	7. don't	7. squirrel
8. they	8. brown	8. thumb
9. train	9. shoe	9. grandmother
10. what	10. light	10. dragon
11. mother	11. hair	11. elephant
12. ride	12. water	12. I'd
13. house	13. own	13. threw
14. new	14. race	14. beautiful
15. here	15. why	15. roof
16. paint	16. hear	16. through
17. work	17. fly	17. leave
18. stop	18. grass	18. unhappy
19. away	19. morning	19. garden
20. around	20. animal	20. branch

THREE	FOUR	FIVE	SIX
1. broom	1. zebra	1. splendor	1. counterclockwise
2. hammer	2. liberty	2. mason	2. diesel
3. log	3. mend	3. radiant	3. mathematical
4. step	4. dolphin	4. cease	4. representative
5. question	5. ability	5. fisherman	5. accomplishment
6. wrinkle	6. compound	6. brief	6. extraordinary
7. invisible	7. gentlemen	7. distress	7. congratulation
8. vegetable	8. holly	8. fake	8. daily
9. engineer	9. swamp	9. false	9. odor
10. allow	10. swarm	10. gust	10. resemble
11. knee	11. chill	11. proceed	11. acquire
12. excitement	12. wreck	12. triumph	12. combine
13. storm	13. solid	13. scuffle	13. opportunity
14. repair	14. alphabet	14. operation	14. transparent
15. sweep	15. holiday	15. military	15. transport
16. swept	16. equal	16. hull	16. cheap
17. million	17. dull	17. genius	17. fifteenth
18. buzz	18. shiver	18. contribution	18. phase
19. doorbell	19. they're	19. reverse	19. violet
20. you've	20. nonsense	20. indicate	20. woolen

Winning the Game

"Catch the ball!" said the girl.

The boy looked at the ball. It came right to him. He did catch it.

"You win the game!" she said.

Growing Up

"When I grow up," said Sally, "I will be big!
My legs and arms will grow. My head will grow.
My face will grow. My nose will grow, too.
What if my nose does not grow? Then my nose
would be a little baby nose on my big face! I would
look funny!"

The Surprise Party

"Hurry," Sue called to all her sisters and brothers. "Hide the balloons and then everybody hide! Don't make a sound or say a word! Dad will be coming home soon!"

When Mr. Brown came into the house, he didn't see his children. All was still, so he didn't hear anything. Then he heard his children laughing, singing, and calling, "Surprise!" He saw many blue, green, and red balloons flying in the air! A big smile grew on his face.

The Soccer Game

I ran down the soccer field kicking the ball.
I was heading straight for the goal. I was close enough
to score. I felt like a million dollars! Wham! I kicked
the ball into the air. It smacked the top of the goalpost
and landed right behind the goal. I really felt rotten!

So, the other team's player got the ball. He looked
like he was ready to power-kick the ball to the moon. Smack!
The ball flew right toward me. I bent my knees low and then
jumped up with all my might. Whack! I hit the ball with my head.
It went jetting straight into the goal. I was truly a soccer hero!

The Baseball Card

The boys got together because it was the afternoon of the great baseball card swap.

"I've got an old timer!" Joe shouted. In his hand he clutched a card that he secretly thought was a loser. It wasn't a popular one like the ones the boys had boasted about all week. Everyone stopped to listen.

No sooner had the words left Joe's mouth than he began to have second thoughts. Like a flash of lightning he remembered when he and his grandfather had gone to the card shop in search of baseball card treasures. He remembered how his grandfather had stood close as they looked through the stacks of cards for endless hours. He remembered the feeling of his grandfather's strong hand on his shoulder.

Joe's face turned flush. In a quiet voice he said, "Oh, never mind! Nobody wants this card because the edges are worn."

The Small Pony

A long time ago a strong horse was important to a farmer, so it was no surprise that Joel's father was storming mad. Mr. Goss had sent Joel to a nearby town to collect some money a man owed him. Joel had returned with a pony instead of the money! The news had spread that the pony was small. People were already laughing. What good was a small pony when there was heavy farm work to do?

Joel hoped to calm his father's anger by telling him about the pony's unusual strength. Mr. Goss would not listen. He pounded his fist on the table shouting several commands! The pony could not stay on his land! In the morning he would take his son to the saw mill and ask if Joel could live and work there. Joel felt shocked and hurt. How could he leave his home and also lose the pony he loved?

A Woman Jockey

"I know that I was last in the race," announced Robyn Smith, "but I am determined to be the best jockey, even if I am a woman!"

It was a rainy morning in 1969, and as Robyn stood outside talking to a horse trainer, Frank Wright, she was so dripping wet that water came running out of the top of her boots. Wright never doubted her ability, and so he gave her a chance to prove herself. One December afternoon Robyn won fourth place in a tough race. People noticed that she had a special way with horses that made them run fast for her.

Then Robyn got another chance. She was to compete against a famous horse named Onion. At race time Robyn mounted her horse, and he nervously pranced back and forth. "Everyone thinks you are wild on the track!" she said in a soft voice. "North Star, you and I will defeat Onion," she said, and he quickly calmed. Then, to everyone's surprise, she won the race. Now the whole world would accept her as an excellent rider.

The First Gas Mask

The explosion was horrible that tragic day in Cleveland, Ohio, in 1916. Thirty-two men were trapped in a tunnel 250 feet below Lake Erie, and no one could enter the smoke-filled atmosphere. "Someone get Garrett Morgan to help!" shouted a man. "Morgan's breathing device is the only thing that can help to rescue the survivors!"

Garrett Morgan and his brother quickly volunteered to assist. "My breathing device will save those victims' lives," Morgan announced with confidence. "I invented it so firemen can breathe when they enter a burning house filled with suffocating gases. We tested my device in an air-tight tent that was filled with the foulest, thickest smoke. A man put my diver's helmet-like device with long breathing tubes running to the floor over his head, went into the tent, stayed twenty minutes, and emerged unharmed!"

Then, Morgan and his brother placed the devices over their heads and rushed into the death-trap tunnel. One by one they carried each man to the surface. Although not every life was spared, it was Morgan's invention, the first gas mask, that saved lives that day and in the years to come.

Dating a Loner

Kate sat in her senior biology class, but she wasn't hearing a single word the teacher was saying because her mind was thoroughly preoccupied. She could think only about Dave and her date with him last Friday night. The entire thing was so confusing and distracting that she kept glancing sideways to where he was sitting near the windows.

He was by far the most handsome boy at Tylerton High. He was tall and strong, with shaggy hair and brilliant blue eyes, but there was something very different about Dave Burdick which she found difficult to accept. She knew that he was independent, and at times actually seemed defiant. She found this disturbing. He always neglected his appearance as if he didn't care what others thought. He was an excellent football player, probably the best in the entire school, but he quit the team. Sometimes he could be stubborn and belligerent, and would argue with anyone over anything.

He never hung around the other kids, so it seemed to her that he was a loner. He drove an old Ford pickup, which had chicken feathers and farm tools scattered all over the floor. Kate felt that he was more interested in raising chickens than in having friends. Yet, even knowing all of these things, she was sure he was a good and decent person. Something crazy was going on in her mind; Dave Burdick was fascinating.

First Day of High School Jitters

"Most ninth graders are a bundle of nerves on the first day of high school, but not me!" Jack Gaither boasted to a group of fellow ninth graders. "I plan on being calm, cool, and collected!" he continued as he thumped his chest. "By the end of day one at Wheaten High School, I will be the most notorious ninth grader!"

The week before school started, Jack meticulously planned each detail. First, he imagined the casual stroll from the school bus; with his head held up, he invented a composed appearance. The most difficult assignment, however, would be to get from his locker to class within three minutes. Dealing with the combination lock had to go flawlessly, so Jack rehearsed how to efficiently spin the knob forward, backward, forward, then smugly lift the latch, and gently swing the door open. "The mission can be accomplished in a minute and a half, leaving plenty of time to nonchalantly saunter into class!" He knew his plan was absolutely comprehensive!

On the first day of school, as Jack emerged from the bus, he tripped over his own feet and propelled forward, knocking three students into each other. Once inside, he lunged toward his locker, twirling the knob so fast that he absentmindedly forgot the combination. Finally, as he yanked the door open, it smacked him in the head. He hustled down the hallway, lowering his head to prevent anyone from noticing the lump that was welling up on his forehead. He edged through the classroom doorway and settled into a seat in the back row.

Abruptly, the bell began clanging, resounding in rhythm with his throbbing head. "This is *Senior English, College Preparation*," the teacher's voice attached itself to the final vibration of the bell. "Well, I recognize all of you except for one student!"

FORM B

Restoring Pigeon Creek

Some time ago Pigeon Creek flowed with transparent, unpolluted water and was a prolific spawning ground for salmon. Then Everett, Washington's population flourished, and for decades to follow, members of the community thoughtlessly dumped debris into the stream. Bottles, aluminum cans, styrofoam cups, old tires, smashed cardboard, rusted bedsprings, ruined refrigerators, and other contaminants choked the once unpolluted water. Erosion occurred from the cutting of trees, causing silt to slide down the embankments. The water turned from transparent to murky, consequently threatening the lives of the fish. Eventually, the fish disappeared; not one had been sighted for twenty years.

The creek's final half-mile runs below Jackson Elementary School and then meanders toward Puget Sound through a culvert, under a railroad track, and finally across a sandy beach as it flows toward the sea. The students and their teachers had studied environmental issues and decided to take a stand. "We want to adopt Pigeon Creek and work to restore its clean water," the president of the student council announced.

"Pigeon Creek is past saving! Maybe you should just forget it!" advised many adults.

Undaunted, the elementary students began working, and "Operation Pigeon Creek" became the slogan for their mission. Guided by their teachers, the students began to extricate the rubbish and to patrol the creek-side to discourage new dumping. They made signs and placed them throughout the community, reminding people not to dump refuse in the creek. Eventually, the students garnered so much public attention that they brought political pressure on the city council and stopped the construction of a storage facility that would have been built near the mouth of the creek.

Then, the school set up an aquarium and stocked it with salmon eggs, and the students accepted the responsibility for maintaining the tank and caring for the eggs. They watched in wonder as the eggs hatched and grew; shortly, they released the young salmon into the creek for their migration to the sea. "Will some eventually return to Pigeon Creek to begin the life-cycle over again?" one student asked as the young salmon wiggled into the water.

Reader's Passages

◼ FORM C ◼

Word Lists and Narrative Passages, Preprimer—Nine

PRIMER	**ONE**	**TWO**
1. about	1. ice	1. goose
2. can	2. before	2. mouse
3. who	3. another	3. library
4. with	4. children	4. teacher
5. some	5. stopped	5. kite
6. goat	6. hurry	6. cart
7. out	7. drop	7. different
8. trees	8. friend	8. anyone
9. father	9. balloon	9. feather
10. red	10. when	10. pie
11. green	11. where	11. sidewalk
12. make	12. those	12. straight
13. is	13. picnic	13. telephone
14. yes	14. laugh	14. clean
15. saw	15. farm	15. remember
16. get	16. airplane	16. wood
17. ball	17. tomorrow	17. summer
18. and	18. wagon	18. bell
19. down	19. made	19. gun
20. are	20. surprise	20. matter

FORM C

THREE	FOUR	FIVE	SIX
1. clap	1. canoe	1. prevent	1. midstream
2. fright	2. hasn't	2. kindle	2. lens
3. diamond	3. dozen	3. grease	3. bail
4. silence	4. motion	4. typical	4. college
5. nurse	5. pride	5. foam	5. failure
6. wiggle	6. vicious	6. blur	6. falter
7. precious	7. concern	7. mumps	7. width
8. salt	8. harvest	8. telegram	8. graceful
9. bread	9. sample	9. vision	9. somewhat
10. breath	10. official	10. sandal	10. privacy
11. fellow	11. windshield	11. argument	11. microphone
12. several	12. human	12. hail	12. particle
13. unusual	13. humor	13. halt	13. clutter
14. overhead	14. decorate	14. region	14. applaud
15. driven	15. slender	15. manager	15. vapor
16. fool	16. seventh	16. sleet	16. reluctant
17. darkness	17. parachute	17. yarn	17. contract
18. honor	18. good-bye	18. parallel	18. nephew
19. screen	19. dignity	19. coconut	19. insurance
20. they'll	20. trudge	20. dissolve	20. fund

FORM C

The Runaway Dog

"I see the dog!" said Dad.
"The dog is running. Now I do not see her.
Where is the dog? Here she is. She has
come back home."

Too Many Animals

I found a lost baby turtle. I took him home to live with me. A friend gave me his rabbit, and I took it home. I found a lost duck. I took her home. Then I saw a cow who looked so sad. I took her home!

Then Mom said, "No, no, not a cow!"

The Show-Off

Jake was playing all by himself outside his house. He
saw a friend from school walk by his yard.
He yelled to him, "Look at me! I can run as fast as a
wild horse! I can jump so high! I can jump over a big,
tall tree! I can ride my bike as fast as a speeding train!
Watch me! I can do it all! I am great. Do you want to
play with me?"

The Busy Road

"Look out, you'll get hit!" I yelled as my dog ran across the busy road. *Thud* was the noise I heard, and then I saw my pup lying in the street. "Oh, no!" I shouted. I felt scared inside. "Rex is my best friend!" I wanted to cry out. I knew that he was hurt, but he'd be all right if I could get help fast. I knew I had to be brave.

"Mom! Dad!" I yelled as I ran straight home. I tried to fight back the tears. They started rolling down my face anyway as I blasted through the door. "Rex has been hit, and he needs help now!" I cried out. "Please hurry so we can save him!"

Belonging to the Club

This was the sign that Jack read as he stood outside the neighborhood kids' clubhouse.

> FOR NEIGHBORHOOD TIGERS ONLY!
> KNOCK ONE HUNDRED TIMES
> AND SAY THE SECRET WORD
> BEFORE ENTERING!

Jack was a new boy, and he really wanted to belong to the club. "How can I get the kids to agree to let me belong?" he thought. Suddenly, he dashed home and soon returned with a bucket of yellow paint, one of black, and several brushes. He began pounding on the clubhouse door.

"I'm knocking one hundred times!" he shouted. "I don't know the secret word," he declared, "but I have something important to tell everyone! I'm the new boy," he explained. "Since the name of your club is *Tigers*, I thought you might want to paint your clubhouse yellow with black stripes!" All the kids thought this was a great idea and quickly invited Jack to belong!

The Beloved Horse

Jody was so worried that she had stayed in the barn all day to take care of her sick horse, Gabe. She thought his condition seemed to be growing worse. His breathing grew louder and harder.

At nightfall, Jody brought a blanket from the house so she could sleep near her beloved animal. In the middle of the night the wind whipped around the barn, rattling windows, and the barn door shook as if it would break into splinters. She had been so exhausted that she slept through all the noise.

When the dawn light poured through the windows, Jody stirred. Bits of straw stuck in her hair and onto her wrinkled clothes. Where was the sound of the sickly breathing? She sat up with a jolt! Then she saw Gabe, healthy and strong, standing by the open door. To her surprise it looked like he was saying, "Let's go for a run!"

FORM C

A Woman Race Car Driver

"I want to be the fastest woman top fuel car driver in the world," stated Shirley Muldowney. "I want to go 500 miles per hour!" In those days, top fuel cars were the fastest, the most powerful, and the most carefully built machines in the car racing sport.

At last the day of Shirley's big race arrived. The engines roared and Shirley blasted forward just like she was the top challenger in the country! It wasn't long before the speedometer read 220 miles per hour, and as Shirley's determination kicked in, the car seemed to propel forward. Her mind raced as she whizzed around the track. "I can accomplish anything I set out to do!" At 230 miles per hour her confidence and her nerves of steel began to push the car faster.

Then, at 242 miles per hour, she established a record speed that no other top fuel driver had reached. Seconds later, her car rushed over the victory line! "Finally," she thought as she pulled into Victory Lane, "now people will think of me as a top race car driver and not just as a woman who drives a race car!"

Open Heart Surgery

It was a hot and humid July day in Chicago in 1893. Tempers flared, and a fight in a saloon ended in a stabbing. "James Cornish has been stabbed in the chest!" shouted one horrified bystander. "Rush him to Provident Hospital, immediately!"

Cornish arrived at the hospital with a one-inch knife wound dangerously near his heart. Dr. Daniel Hale Williams was called in to operate. After an examination, Williams found that the knife had indeed cut the heart as well as the sac around the heart, so he knew he had to work swiftly. In those days chest surgery was rarely attempted because blood transfusions and antibiotics were unknown. Open heart surgery was an invitation to death. "Would infection set in and kill the patient? Should I risk my reputation?" Williams must have been thinking. The atmosphere in the operating room was tense as six other physicians prepared to observe this daring surgery.

Fifty-one days after Cornish came to the hospital a dying man, he was discharged a well man! In fact, he lived for fifty years after his surgery and even outlived Dr. Daniel Hale Williams by twelve years.

Broken Friendship

Jim was sixteen years old, and he thought more of his older brother Kevin than anyone else. In Jim's opinion, Kevin was the greatest guy in the entire world. He was certain it would be a terrific summer because he believed it would be an opportunity for a genuine brother-to-brother reunion. He had informed all his friends that he was going to spend the total summer with Kevin.

When Kevin arrived home from his first year at college, he was a different person. He had new friends, attitudes, and interests that gave Jim an uneasy feeling. Kevin wasn't interested in talking to Jim about old times. When Jim tried to talk to him, Kevin seemed disinterested, making Jim feel like he was talking to a brick wall. When the phone rang, Kevin rushed to answer it, then strolled down the hallway, closing the door behind him. It wasn't long before Jim felt rejected like an outcast being shoved away.

Before Kevin went away, they had a tight relationship. As far back as Jim could remember, they drove the long fifteen miles from the farm to school together. When Jim was a freshman in high school, Kevin was a senior, and they attended every sport event as a pair—no one could separate them. They told each other jokes and laughed just like super buddies. Jim could still feel Kevin's brotherly smack on his shoulder that always went with these words, "Well, okay, Little Brother, as partners we make up a superior team!" Now, Jim felt like a side liner. Was he going to be an outsider forever?

The Science Project

Janice Cornwell was a top-notch student, so when the eighth grade science projects were assigned, all the other students in the class glowered at Janice because they knew her grade would be an A+. Jason Crawford often heckled, "Janice is going to get an A+++!"

Janice wanted to do research on nutrition. She planned to purchase three guinea pigs and over a two-month period prepare meals containing different amounts of protein. One guinea pig would get a diet with protein-rich foods, another got the same food plus protein supplements, and the last guinea pig would get minimal amounts of protein. She named the three laboratory animals after famous scholars: Plato, Socrates, and Da Vinci. "I'll gather data by observing the quality of their fur and the energy level of each research guinea pig. The procedure is sound and everything is scientifically factual!"

After two weeks something happened that didn't figure on the data chart. Plato, whose coat was getting thick and fluffy, liked to be petted; Socrates, whose coat was less thick and less fluffy, liked to cuddle; and poor little Da Vinci, whose coat was getting scraggly, liked his stomach scratched. Unexpectedly, this scientific experiment was turning from a data-gathering event into a labor of love.

On the day the projects were due, students came to school carrying cages, large charts, and final reports. The science teacher told everyone to set their projects on the counters in alphabetical order. Janice refused to set her cage on the counter. She wasn't about to place it near Jason Crawford's boa constrictor experiment. "I don't have any data and I don't have a final report!" she announced. Stunned, everyone turned toward Janice. "How can I experiment on my pets?"

FORM C

The Urban Garden

"Once this corner was the neighborhood garbage dump!" Malinda Futrell said as she briskly swung open the chain-link gate leading to an urban garden situated on the corner of Sixth Street and Avenue B in New York City. To a passerby this luscious corner of green, thriving amid city air laden with exhaust fumes, cement dust, and general urban pollution, is an unexpected sight. Yet the sunlight that squeezes between the towering apartment buildings casts the gift of light on flourishing plots of vegetables, flowers, and fruit. Here, 105 enthusiastic neighborhood urban gardeners cultivate the soil and create a touch of rural life amid the noise and bustle of city life.

Several years ago, Joanee Freedom, now one of the neighborhood's avid gardeners, noticed a tomato plant growing amid the mounds of trash. "How could a small plant survive those wretched conditions?" she wondered. "I was so intrigued that I trudged through the rubbish, brushed the debris from the remarkable specimen, and built a small protective brick wall around it! Then within a short period of time, another neighbor noticed the extraordinary plant. The next thing I knew, he'd cleared a small plot and planted his own garden."

The small garden looked conspicuous in contrast to the surrounding litter, and it was this little expression of individuality that launched Malinda Futrell into a plan that eventually grew into the Sixth Street and Avenue B Garden Project. A native of North Carolina, Malinda had moved to the city only to find herself yearning for the land she'd left behind. "What was I doing here with all this noise and cement and no soil to dig my hands into?" she pined. Within a matter of days after seeing the small garden, Malinda secured permission from the city government to create a neighborhood Victory Garden. She promptly began clearing the rubble and cultivating the soil. Now, as a city dweller hustles past the corner of Sixth Street and Avenue B, plots of vegetables, meadows of wildflowers, and corners of fragrant herbs fill the sight and other senses.

Reader's Passages
▣ FORM S ▣
Expository Science Passages, One—Nine

The Five Senses

We have five senses. They help us learn. We can learn about color if we can see. We can hear our name called out if we can hear. We can feel a soft, warm kitten if we can touch it with our hands. We can smell good things if we can smell. We can taste the salt in the sea if we can taste. Our lives would change if we did not have all five senses. It would be a lot harder to learn.

Hearing Sounds

Sounds can be made in many ways. Sound is made if someone hits a drum or shakes a paper.

We say something vibrates when it moves back and forth. As something vibrates back and forth, it makes the air around it move. The moving air is called a sound wave. Sound waves move through the air. Ears can hear sound waves.

A bell begins to vibrate if someone hits the bell. The air around the bell vibrates, too. The sound waves go through the air. Small parts inside the ears begin to vibrate. The ears hear the sound. Ears can hear soft or loud sounds. Ears can hear high or low sounds, and they can hear fuzzy or clear sounds.

Changing Matter

We call an object matter if it takes up space. All things around you are called matter because they have size, shape, and weight. Houses, school desks, flowers, and kangaroos are all matter. People are matter, too.

A rock, milk, and air are matter. Each one is different even though each is matter. Each has its own size, shape, and weight. A rock is a solid. Milk is a liquid. Air is a gas. Matter can take different forms. It can be a solid, a liquid, or a gas.

Matter can change from one form to another. Ice is a solid. Ice can become a liquid called water if it is heated. Water can become a gas called steam if it is heated. Steam can become a liquid if it is cooled. Water can become a solid called ice if it is cooled.

A Comet

A long time ago people became frightened when they saw a comet. They thought a comet was a sign that unpleasant events, such as an earthquake, would take place. Scientists now know that these ideas are not correct.

A comet is a space object made up of ice particles mixed with dust. Comets probably come from the far, outer edge of our solar system. Comets can be seen only when they are close enough to the sun to reflect its light.

A comet has two parts: the head and the tail. The tail is present only when the comet is heated by the sun. The tail is made of fine dust and gas. A comet's tail always points away from the sun. It can be millions of kilometers long. The head is made of ice, frozen gases, and particles of rock and metal. It could be described as a dirty snowball. The heads of most comets are only a few kilometers wide. As they near the sun, reflected sunlight makes them appear large.

From *Accent on Science, Level 4*, Merrill Publishing Company, 1985, page 104.
Reprinted, here and in the Examiner's Record, with permission of the publisher.

FORMS

Worms: Parasites and Scavengers

Worms that live inside the bodies of other animals are parasites. Parasites are living things that feed on other living things. When some meat, such as pork, is not cooked long enough, even people can get worms by eating the meat. The worms attach themselves to the intestines, where they absorb food. Soon people who have parasites may lose weight and become weak. It is important to cook meat well.

Flatworms are the simplest worms. They have one body opening and a digestive system with intestines. Some flatworms are scavengers. Scavengers are animals that eat dead animals. The flatworm planarian is a scavenger. Other flatworms are parasites.

Roundworms are more complex than flatworms. They have two body openings, not one. The openings are connected by a long intestine. Food enters the mouth and wastes leave from the opposite opening.

Segmented worms are the most complex type of worm. Their bodies are divided into small parts, or segments. Two body openings are connected by a long intestine. They have a heart-like organ. It pumps blood through blood vessels. They even have a small brain in the front part of their bodies. A nerve cord runs the length of their bodies.

From *Accent on Science, Level 5,* Merrill Publishing Company, 1985, pages 27–28.
Reprinted, here and in the Examiner's Record, with permission of the publisher.

FORM S

Disease Microbes and Antibodies

Your body has many natural ways to prevent disease microbes from causing infections. For instance, your skin is a barrier for microbes. They seldom pass through unbroken skin. The hairs in your nose filter some microbes out of the air you breathe. Also, there are some other ways disease microbes are kept from entering your body.

Sometimes disease microbes do enter your body. Often when you have an infection caused by disease microbes, your body makes antibodies. An antibody is a chemical produced in your blood to destroy certain microbes. Your body makes a different kind of antibody for each kind of disease microbe.

Perhaps you have been sick with chicken pox. Chicken pox is caused by a microbe infection. When you got chicken pox, your body began making antibodies to destroy the microbes. As the microbes were destroyed by the antibodies, you began to get well. Antibodies stay in your blood even after you no longer have the disease. They keep you from getting that disease again. For this reason most people have a disease like chicken pox only once.

Vaccines are used to help your body make certain antibodies. A vaccine is made of dead or weak microbes that cause a certain disease. When a vaccine is put into your body, you do not get the disease.

From *Accent on Science, Level 6,* Merrill Publishing Company, 1985, pages 19–20.
Reprinted, here and in the Examiner's Record, with permission of the publisher.

FORMS

Moving Forces and Inertia

Without motion the hands of a clock would not indicate the time of day. For every motion there is a force that causes it. A force is needed to start something moving or to change its direction. A force is also needed to stop motion. The tendency of matter to stay at rest or in motion unless acted on by a force is called inertia.

A person riding in a car has inertia. Think of a car moving at a speed of 50 kilometers per hour. How fast is the person inside going? The person is moving with the car and is not left behind; therefore, the person must also be moving at 50 kilometers per hour. If the brakes are applied suddenly, what happens to the person in the car? The person continues to move forward even though the car is stopping. If the seatbelt is unfastened, the dashboard or windshield may stop this forward motion.

If you are standing in a bus, you may be thrown off balance when the bus starts to move. Your body has inertia. It tends to remain in place as the bus begins to move. If the bus goes forward too fast, you may fall backward.

All matter has inertia. Inertia is a property of matter. The amount of inertia an object has depends on its mass. The greater the mass of an object, the greater its inertia. A sofa of large mass has more inertia than a kitchen chair. It takes more force to move a sofa than to move a kitchen chair. It takes a larger force to start and stop a bus than to start and stop a small sports car.

From *Principles of Science, Book Two*, Glencoe/McGraw-Hill Publishing, 1986, pages 107–108. Reprinted, here and in the Examiner's Record, with permission of the publisher.

FORM S

Cancer

Cancer is a disease in which there is abnormal cell division and a rapid increase in certain body cells. Cancer can occur in any plant or animal. Dogs, cats, fruit flies, and horses, as well as humans, can develop various types of cancer. What causes the abnormal rapid growth of body cells? The DNA of a cell nucleus controls the growth and division of the cell. Normal cells grow to a certain size. For some unknown reason, some cells may continue to grow and divide. This rapid growth of cells leads to a formation of a clump of tissue called a tumor. A benign, non-life-threatening tumor will grow to a certain size and stop. Most moles and warts are benign tumors. All malignant tumors are cancers. They can cause death if they are not removed or destroyed. Cancer cells, unlike normal cells, may separate from a tumor and be carried through the blood or lymph to other organs of the body. They can invade a new body tissue and form new tumors.

Cancer in many animals is known to be caused by viruses. Chickens are affected by a cancer of the connective tissue. Epstein-Barr viruses cause cancer of the lymph system in humans. Scientists are working to discover how viruses cause cancer.

A carcinogen is a cancer-causing substance. Many different chemicals are known to be carcinogens. Certain chemicals in the environment can cause cancer. Nitrosamines, reaction products of sodium nitrate, are carcinogens. Sodium nitrate is used to preserve meat. The nitrosamines are produced during the digestive process. Too much sunlight and overexposure to X-rays and other radiation can be physical causes of cancer.

FORMS

From *Principles of Science, Book Two,* Glencoe/McGraw-Hill Publishing, 1986, pages 128–129. Reprinted, here and in the Examiner's Record, with permission of the publisher.

Knowing the Atom

About 2,300 years ago, the Greek philosopher Democritus proposed the idea that matter is composed of atoms. Democritus reasoned that an apple could be cut into smaller and smaller pieces. Eventually he would have particles that could no longer be cut and still be an apple. He called these small particles "atoms," which is Greek for "unable to cut."

Democritus never saw an atom. Atoms are too small for anyone to view directly. For example, one drop of water contains millions of atoms. Scientists often propose models to help them visualize things that they cannot see directly. These models are based on scientific theories. Much of the early work in atomic theory was done in England. The Cavendish Laboratory at the University of Cambridge was the site of many important discoveries about atomic structure. As more information was gathered by scientists about atoms, the atomic theory was revised. Scientists are still learning about atoms and atomic structure.

According to current atomic theory, the atom consists of a small, dense nucleus surrounded by mostly empty space in which electrons move at high speeds. Most of an atom's volume is empty space. The average diameter of a nucleus is about 5×10^{-13} centimeters. The average diameter of an atom is about 2×10^{-8} centimeters. The difference in these two sizes means an atom is about 40,000 times larger than its nucleus. Consider an example of this relative difference. If the nucleus were the size of an orange, the whole atom would measure twenty-four city blocks across.

Even though an atomic nucleus is relatively small, it makes up over 99.9 percent of an atom's mass. The nucleus of an atom contains protons. A proton is a relatively massive particle with a positive electric charge. The nucleus of a helium atom contains two protons. The mass of a helium atom is about twice the mass of two protons. The additional mass is due to neutrons found in the nuclei of the helium atoms. A neutron is a nuclear particle that has no electric charge. A neutron has about the same mass as a proton. Most atomic nuclei contain neutrons.

From *Merrill General Science,* Merrill Publishing Company, 1986, pages 71–72. Reprinted, here and in the Examiner's Record, with permission of the publisher.

Reader's Passages

◼ FORM SS ◼

Expository Social Studies
Passages, One—Nine

Our Country's Flag

Our country's flag is red, white, and blue. The colors come from the flag of England. The stars and stripes on our flag have a special meaning. The thirteen red and white stripes stand for our first thirteen states. Each star stands for one of our fifty states.

Our flag stands for the past. Our flag also stands for the present. It stands for a free nation. It stands for our country. It stands for the United States of America.

The First Thirteen States

Over 300 years ago, the English started thirteen colonies. Later, the colonies became the first states in the United States of America. The people in the first states had difficult lives. For transportation they often walked. Sometimes they rode horses. It was hard for the people to travel very far from home because there were no cars.

The people's houses were much different from our houses today. The houses had one large room with a fireplace. This room was used as a kitchen, a dining room, and a living room. Also, it was often used as a bedroom because of the fireplace. There were no electric lights. Water had to be carried into the house. Even though life was very difficult, the people worked hard because they loved their new land.

Writing the *Declaration of Independence*

During the middle 1760s, American colonists became more and more unhappy with the king of England. They were unhappy because he took away their right to freedom. They were unhappy because he took so much of their money for taxes.

In 1776, men from the thirteen colonies met in Philadelphia. Some men believed that the colonies should separate from England. These men thought the colonies should be free, even if it meant war.

One of the men at the meeting was Thomas Jefferson. Jefferson had read many books about government and law. He did not speak much during the meeting, but he listened carefully. He thought about the reasons for freedom.

Later, Jefferson wrote something that told why the colonists should be free. The other men liked what Jefferson had written. On July 4th, the men voted to accept Jefferson's work. They called it the *Declaration of Independence,* and then the war for freedom became fierce.

French Explorers in North America

During the 1600s, the French settled much of eastern Canada. They called this land New France. They had heard stories about a large body of water to the west. The French thought it might be the Pacific Ocean. They wanted more land to add to the French Empire. Soon they began to look for the great body of water. This journey took them to regions that are now part of the United States. Some went south instead of west.

In 1679, a Frenchman, La Salle, began a second journey to explore the Great Lakes region. He started at the south end of Lake Michigan. He followed the Illinois River to the place where it met the Mississippi River. By 1682, he had gone all the way down the Mississippi to where it flowed into the Gulf of Mexico. He claimed the lands on both sides of the river. He also claimed the rivers that flowed into the land. He named the region Louisiana in honor of Louis XIV, the French king.

The Civil War

During the early and mid-1800s, there was much talk in the United States about slavery. Most of the northern states had outlawed slavery. However, in the South, slaves were considered important to the plantation owners who grew cotton and tobacco. The slavery issue was not settled until Abraham Lincoln was elected president in 1860.

Until 1861 all the states had worked together as the United States. However, in 1861, leaders in the southern states believed that states had the right to leave, or secede from, the United States. The leaders in the northern and western states believed that no state had the right to secede. This difference in beliefs was one cause of the Civil War.

The states that seceded from the Union were states that used slaves. Those states formed a group called the Confederate States of America, or simply, the Confederacy. When the Civil War began in 1861, there were eleven southern states in the Confederacy.

The Civil War was very difficult because Americans were fighting Americans. In some cases brothers fought on opposing sides. After four long years of fighting, the South surrendered in April of 1865.

How the Industrial Revolution Changed the Textile Industry

In the late 1700s in the United States, the Industrial Revolution was making rapid changes in the way people lived. One of history's stories of how lives changed was told in the growth of the textile industry. Textile is woven or knitted cloth.

For hundreds of years before the Industrial Revolution, farm families had spun yarn or thread and then woven the cloth. This was done in their homes. It was one way they could earn extra money. Oftentimes, a whole family would help to make the cloth. Merchants who wanted cloth to sell in their shops supplied a family with the raw goods like wool or cotton.

In 1733, an Englishman named John Kay invented the flying shuttle, which helped weavers work more quickly. In 1764, James Hargreaves invented the spinning jenny. His invention could produce eight threads at once instead of only one. Finally, a power loom was invented.

Soon the new machines became so big and cost so much that a family could not afford them. Also, they needed to be located near some kind of power source. Buildings called factories were built near fast-moving streams. Instead of spinning cloth in the farm homes, workers had to leave their homes. They traveled to the factories and worked long hours away from home.

The Birth of Public Education and Leisure Time

In the 1870s, some states turned their attention to public education. They passed compulsory attendance laws. These laws required that children attend school for a certain part of the year. By 1900, thirty states had passed such laws.

More people turned their attention to higher education during the late 1800s. One of the reasons for this was the Morrill Act, passed in 1862. Under this act, states were given public lands to set up state colleges of engineering, teacher training, and agriculture. Meanwhile, the total number of colleges grew from about 500 in 1870 to nearly 1,000 in 1900. During these years, educational opportunities increased for both women and blacks. By 1900, nearly 100,000 women were attending college. Also, blacks had founded over thirty colleges, mostly in the South. Over 2,000 black students had graduated from these colleges.

The growing interest in education was matched by a growing amount of time spent at leisure. Greater use of labor-saving machines both at work and at home made it possible for people to have more free time. This free time was spent in a number of ways. Americans spent a great deal of time at sports. The most popular spectator sport was baseball. In 1869, the first professional team, the Cincinnati Red Stockings, was formed. In 1876, teams from eight cities formed the National League, and in 1900, the American League was set up. The first World Series, between the Boston Red Sox and the Pittsburgh Pirates, was played in 1903.

Football was nearly as popular a spectator sport as baseball. It had first been played between teams of students from the same college. Then in 1869, the first intercollegiate (involving two or more colleges) game took place between Princeton and Rutgers.

From *America Is,* Merrill Publishing Company, 1987, pages 457–458. Reprinted, here and in the Examiner's Record, with permission of the publisher.

FORM SS

The Vietnam War

In 1955, American advisers had been sent to South Vietnam to train the army. Both Presidents Eisenhower and Kennedy sent more advisers, support troops, and military supplies between 1956 and 1962.

By the time Lyndon Johnson became president, a group of South Vietnamese Communists, called the Viet Cong, were well established in South Vietnam. They fought as guerrillas—bands who make war by harassment and sabotage. The Viet Cong were getting help from North Vietnam.

In August 1964, after an attack by North Vietnamese gunboats on American warships in the Gulf of Tonkin, President Johnson asked Congress to allow him to take steps to prevent future attacks. Congress replied by passing the Tonkin Gulf Resolution. It allowed the President, as Commander in Chief, to use any measure necessary to halt an attack on American forces, stop North Vietnamese aggression, and aid any SEATO member who asked for help defending its freedom.

In February 1965, Viet Cong attacks killed several Americans. This led President Johnson to order the bombing of North Vietnam. The President also sent the first combat troops to South Vietnam. By the end of 1968, there were more than 500,000 American soldiers there. The war was costing the United States about $25 billion a year.

Public opinion was divided over the Vietnam War. Many people felt that the war was necessary to stop communism. Others felt that it was a civil war that should be settled by the Vietnamese. Still others felt that the money spent on the war could be put to better use at home. These divisions were seen in Congress, which was divided between the "hawks"—those who favored greater military effort—and the "doves"—those who wanted the war effort lessened.

From *America Is*, Merrill Publishing Company, 1987, pages 656–657. Reprinted, here and in the Examiner's Record, with permission of the publisher.

Knowing the American Economy

In recent years, the American economy has been changing. It has been growing steadily. The gross national product (GNP), the value of all goods and services produced in one year, rose. In 1950, the GNP was $286 billion. In 1984, it was $3.6 trillion. This growth, aided by new technology, has affected the labor force and farming. Nevertheless, there are problems with the economy that need to be corrected. One thing that has helped change the American economy is technology— application of ideas, methods, and tools to the production of goods. Technology has helped Americans make more goods with less work. It has also helped Americans raise their standard of living, and it has given them more leisure time.

One example of the new technology is automation, the making of products by machines that are controlled electronically. For example, machines can be used to weld parts of cars together and to print newspapers. Machines that are run by only one or two people can roll and shape steel. However, automation eliminates the need for certain jobs. This means fewer jobs and more people out of work.

Another example of the new technology is computerization. Computers were first developed in the 1950s, but they were large and expensive. During the 1960s, scientists replaced bulky tubes with small transistors, and computers became smaller and less expensive. They were used by banks, hospitals, and businesses to store and file vast amounts of information. In the 1970s, computers became even smaller when they were powered by microchips, tiny chips of silicon smaller than a postage stamp. Soon, doctors, lawyers, housewives, students, and others were able to buy their own computers. Now, many schools and colleges require their students to own a personal computer.

Problems with foreign trade affect the economy. Over time, the United States has imported more resources, such as oil, along with a growing number of manufactured goods. Cars, radios, cameras, and hundreds of other items made in other countries are sold to Americans every year. So much has been sold that the United States has a poor balance of trade.

From *America Is,* Merrill Publishing Company, 1987, page 732. Reprinted, here and in the Examiner's Record, with permission of the publisher.

Reader's Passages